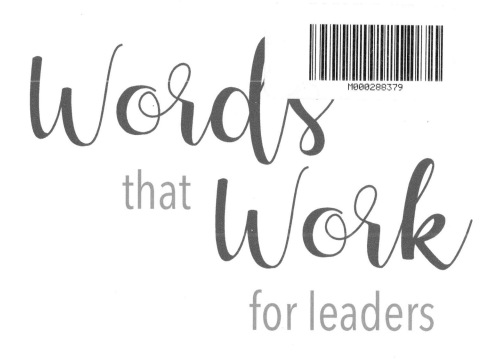

Words that Work for leaders

31 days of reflection, motivation, and goal setting.

written by **LAURA BOYD**   designed by **KRISTIN HARTUNG**

ISBN: 978-1-7345829-3-2

Library of Congress Control Number: 2020919719

Published in the United States of America by the Write Place, Inc.
For more information please contact:

the Write Place, Inc.
809 W. 8th Street, Suite 2
Pella, Iowa 50219
www.thewriteplace.biz

Cover and interior design by Kristin Hartung.

View other Write Place titles at www.thewriteplace.biz.

I often ask people when they first realized that they were a leader. For many reasons, people tend to struggle to recall an example – maybe it was too long ago, or perhaps there are too many examples to choose from. Maybe they have difficulty seeing themselves as a leader. However, despite these difficulties in recognizing the quality of leadership in themselves, people seldom have the same problem when asked to describe traits of the most significant leaders in their lives.

It is a pattern that I've noticed over many years of working with leaders of all kinds at all levels. There are a handful of essential traits that distinguish great leaders from the rest of the pack. Time and again, when experienced professionals are asked to describe the most memorable and impactful leaders in their lives, the same traits appear over and over.

The traits we cover in this book are the same ones that great leaders possess. Since leadership is about who you are as a person and how you live your values, we believe that outstanding leadership is like a muscle that can be strengthened and must be regularly exercised.

After all, we cannot just think new thoughts and expect our lives to change. We must take appropriate, mindful action. We must also have a goal or initiative behind our actions.

The following words of the day were developed in early 2020 when COVID-19 was just beginning its rampant global spread. When there was so much uncertainty and unrest, we found that these words gave us and others a sense of positivity and clear-eyed optimism. They also imbued us with a sense of control in our lives in a world rife with conflict by challenging us with a goal that encouraged us to look inward and reflect on our leadership style. We hope that these words continue to provide the support that leaders will need on their journey to lift others up as they become the best leader possible.

We have done the heavy lifting to help you commit to these goal examples and provide the framework for building your own. You will find small, potential goals on every page of *Words that Work for Leaders* that encourage you to think about your leadership style.

In the spaces provided, write down what you believe your strengths are and where you have the opportunity to develop. When you look at that list, what do you notice? How do you feel about some of those words? Which traits are you most proud of, and what do you wish you had more of?

Please do not skip this step of writing down your responses. Research shows that when we write down our goals, we have a better chance of success. Get your thoughts and plans on paper or in pixels!

Whenever you embark on changing an aspect of your life, your first step is the same as an athlete's when she is headed to training from the minor to the major. Specifically, you need to warm up and strengthen your muscles. In this case, your muscle is your brain. There are a few critical mindfulness practices that will keep your muscle focused and healthy:

Awareness.
Desire.
Commitment.
Practice.

Awareness

Awareness is about responding to life rather than reacting to it. It becomes about the choices we make to be our best selves. Developing your leadership skills calls for you to become purposefully more aware of yourself and your motivations. Meaning, you need to discover your "why" to make meaningful, lasting progress. Are you working on your leadership skills to become a better manager? To be promoted or to find a new job? Are you trying to be your best self out in the community? Do you want to focus on being more present with your family?

Once you've discovered your "why," you will be able to have a heightened awareness of your feelings, thoughts, and emotions. Even more powerful, you will be able to change the stories that you tell yourself. If you've been following a destructive script that's kept you back from becoming the best leader possible, developing your awareness is key to stopping it.

Desire

Your next step is to cultivate your desire to embark on a journey of change. If you have a strong desire to respond to life instead of merely reacting to it, you must have the desire to make that happen. Right about now, you might be thinking that desire sounds an awful lot like awareness, but there is one key difference: your desire can only come from YOU. You cannot outsource it, and you cannot set daily reminders to desire to change.

Commitment

Before setting off in earnest on your journey, you need to create and implement a plan. Share with a supportive community that you intend to improve and develop your leadership skills. Also, be careful about falling into the destructive mindset of telling yourself that you "cannot" change. The words we use on ourselves are potent. When you commit to becoming a better leader, your change begins with the language you use. Turn "I can't" into the commitment statement of "I choose not to," and you will see that you have much more power than you previously thought.

Practice

Finally, all of these components depend on deliberate practice to become their most robust. Deliberate practice is about doing the same thing repeatedly, identifying and addressing weaknesses over and over until the desired result becomes a habit. Aristotle once said, "We are what we repeatedly do. Excellence, then, is not an act, but a habit."

However, don't forget that with all great practice, there will come small failures. Failure is a part of every journey to success, as are significant challenges. Have grace and compassion for yourself when these obstacles arise, and you will see that the small failures lead to great lessons.

One more thing: reflection is key to all learning. As you move through these daily words, keep in mind that it's not about the number of words you get down on the page. It is crucial to your journey to genuinely reflect on what the word means to you and what you have to be grateful for. I'll be honest, some days I write a lot, while I can only muster a few things in my gratitude list on other days.

Grace

In times of need or change, giving grace can bring calm
to an otherwise uncomfortable situation.

GOAL

Offer up grace, comfort, and support today to someone
having a difficult time – it may even be you.

MY COMMITMENT

I choose to..._____

_____

_____

_____

_____

I am grateful for..._____

_____

_____

_____

_____

_____

INFLUENCE

Our children are watching. Our teams at work are watching.
As a leader, be the best example of a source of
strength and calm while offering clarity.

GOAL

Act intentionally in front of those that you may influence today,
show them the way to a peaceful mind and an encouraging heart.

MY COMMITMENT

I choose to... _____

_____

_____

_____

_____

I am grateful for... _____

_____

_____

_____

_____

_____

Kindness

In a world where you can be anything, be kind.
It's that simple.

GOAL

Intentionally put something positive out into the world today,
whether it be on social media, via email, or over the phone.

MY COMMITMENT

I choose to..._____

_____

_____

_____

_____

_____

I am grateful for..._____

_____

_____

_____

_____

_____

Calm

A sense of peace. Be mindful today of the
energy you exude to others.

GOAL

Be intentional in the way you handle each positive and
negative situation that comes your way today. Show compassion and
find peace in the negative. Be grateful for the positive.

MY COMMITMENT

I choose to..._____

_____

_____

_____

_____

I am grateful for..._____

_____

_____

_____

_____

_____

UNITY

If we come together in times of need, we all feel whole.

GOAL

Reach out to a group of people that have something in common today, bring an idea that will suit everyone's needs and offer support in bringing the idea to reality.

MY COMMITMENT

I choose to... _____

_____

_____

_____

_____

I am grateful for... _____

_____

_____

_____

_____

_____

Courage

Be brave. Be strong. Be fearless.

GOAL
Take a small leap of faith today,
do something even slightly outside of your comfort zone
and bask in the glory of your tenacity.

MY COMMITMENT

I choose to... _____

_____

_____

_____

_____

I am grateful for... _____

_____

_____

_____

_____

_____

Humanity

Show energy and positive influence for those that
might need it more than you do today. Humanize yourself
and lift them up. Let's come together and reinforce
that we are all in this together.

GOAL
When you encounter someone that is in need of
some support, whether you know them well or not,
offer them encouraging words of strength.

MY COMMITMENT

I choose to... _____

_____

_____

_____

_____

I am grateful for... _____

_____

_____

_____

_____

_____

Harmony

Let's agree on coming together for the common good.

GOAL

Reconnect with someone you haven't spoken
to in a while and see how they are doing.

MY COMMITMENT

I choose to... _____

_____

_____

_____

_____

I am grateful for... _____

_____

_____

_____

_____

_____

Persuade

As we watch and listen to the media there is a lot of information swirling around. Be the positive influence that our world might lack today.

GOAL

Intentionally put something positive out into the world today, whether it be on social media, via email, or over the phone.

MY COMMITMENT

I choose to..._____

_____

_____

_____

_____

I am grateful for... _____

_____

_____

_____

_____

Teamwork

We've all been given gifts to support each other, our team, or our organization towards one vision. Make sure your team knows the vision and help them along the way.

GOAL

Take one opportunity that you can offer a suggestion on and send it to your team (the team might be your family unit) and find resolution together to ensure you have a well-oiled machine.

MY COMMITMENT

I choose to... _____

_____

_____

_____

_____

I am grateful for... _____

_____

_____

_____

_____

Confidence

You are you and you are enough.
Today and every day lift yourself up with words of affirmation.

GOAL

Start today by looking in the mirror and telling yourself
you are worthy of anything you believe to be true.

MY COMMITMENT

I choose to... _____

_____

_____

_____

_____

I am grateful for... _____

_____

_____

_____

_____

Perseverance

Questioning ourselves sometimes comes too easily.
Come to a decision and settle on a purpose.

GOAL

Today, have the determination to conquer
a difficult task. No task is too big or too small,
just accomplish the task at hand.

MY COMMITMENT

I choose to... _____

_____

_____

_____

_____

I am grateful for... _____

_____

_____

_____

_____

_____

Connect

As humans, we are meant to and
need to connect with each other.

GOAL

Today seek out five people outside of your family,
to connect with in person or virtually.

MY COMMITMENT

I choose to... _____

_____

_____

_____

_____

I am grateful for... _____

_____

_____

_____

_____

Compassion

When we show compassion for ourselves
and others, change is happening.

GOAL
Lift someone up daily with words
of love and encouragement.

MY COMMITMENT

I choose to... _____

_____

_____

_____

_____

I am grateful for... _____

_____

_____

_____

_____

_____

Trustworthy

We need to give trust first. We see what we look for.
Directly telling your team or family members
that you trust them allows them to feel
empowered to move forward.

GOAL

Find an instance where your skepticism would
normally creep in; instead offer trust by sharing
that you believe in their idea or motives.

MY COMMITMENT

I choose to... _____

_____

_____

_____

_____

I am grateful for... _____

_____

_____

_____

_____

_____

Listen

As titled leaders, it is easy to get caught up
in the "I Know Best" philosophy due
to frustration or lack of time.

GOAL

Stop. Listen intently. It will mean more in five years
that you listened than getting a project done perfectly.

MY COMMITMENT

I choose to..._____

_____

_____

_____

_____

_____

I am grateful for... _____

_____

_____

_____

_____

_____

Perspective

Throughout our experiences, we see the world
through certain paradigms (fear, duty, achievement, integrity).
Be cognizant of which paradigm you are making a decision
through or how you respond to a team or family member.

GOAL

Recognize a time where you would normally
respond out of fear and shift gears. If you saw the world through a
different paradigm, how would you respond?

MY COMMITMENT

I choose to... _____

_____

_____

_____

_____

_____

I am grateful for... _____

_____

_____

_____

_____

_____

Vulnerable

Trust begins with being vulnerable.
It doesn't matter your title, position, or family status,
you don't always have the answers.

GOAL

Find two instances where you don't have the
answer and share them with your team or family.
Give yourself permission to share
your vulnerabilities.

MY COMMITMENT

I choose to... _____

_____

_____

_____

_____

_____

I am grateful for... _____

_____

_____

_____

_____

_____

HUMOR

In the heaviest and most uncertain of times, find the light.
Laughter produces protective hormones, regulates blood pressure,
reduces the effects of stress and helps boost the immune system. It is even
believed to increase your number of years on this earth by eight!

GOAL

Be intentional about showcasing your smile today.
See if you can intentionally find eight times to smile with or at someone.
How did they respond back?

MY COMMITMENT

I choose to..._____

_____

_____

_____

_____

I am grateful for... _____

_____

_____

_____

_____

_____

Empower

When human beings are empowered,
they become stronger and more confident in their daily tasks.
They are also happier and more at peace with the decisions
they make on behalf of your organization because
they will know you trust in them.

GOAL

Make the intentional decision to empower one or
more of your team members today. Validate the trust you have
in them and their abilities to succeed.

MY COMMITMENT

I choose to... _____

_____

_____

_____

_____

I am grateful for... _____

_____

_____

_____

_____

_____

Purpose

We need a purpose to wake up every day.
Some people refer to this as their True North or their "why."
The purpose is your guide and inner core to
reaching your ultimate goals in life.

GOAL

Using the spiral method, ask yourself "why am I doing this?"
three times to seek your sense of personal purpose.

MY COMMITMENT

I choose to... _____

_____

_____

_____

_____

_____

I am grateful for... _____

_____

_____

_____

_____

_____

Vision

Most people wouldn't take off on a road trip
without a clear vision for where they wanted to end up.
The road to getting there may not be well-defined,
but the ultimate outcome is.

GOAL

Develop a new vision for your organization,
team, family, and self. It may even be a temporary vision
but create it and communicate it often with all
those who are a part of it.

MY COMMITMENT

I choose to... _____

_____

_____

_____

_____

I am grateful for... _____

_____

_____

_____

_____

_____

Adaptable

We KNOW how to be adaptable.
We may push against it, but we CAN adapt. It's a choice.

GOAL

Think of changes where you've adapted that you want to
keep as a new norm. What are two adaptations that you
will keep and one that you will leave behind?

MY COMMITMENT

I choose to..._____

_____

_____

_____

_____

I am grateful for... _____

_____

_____

_____

_____

Consistent

As a leader it is imperative to show consistency.
It lends expectations to your team or family and allows
you to move towards your goal to be held accountable.
During times of chaos or crisis, consistency can be a challenge.
Keep that in mind and be vulnerable when
your consistency shifts.

GOAL

What consistent behaviors do you need to have to reach
your vision? Often, these are the small behavior changes.

MY COMMITMENT

I choose to..._____

_____

_____

_____

_____

_____

I am grateful for..._____

_____

_____

_____

_____

_____

_____

Growth

Growth comes in all forms, shapes, and sizes. Leaders need to have and instill a growth mindset. Their willingness to fail and be vulnerable will allow them to build trust with their teams, organizations, and families.

GOAL

Find something you've wanted to try and go for it with the willingness to fail and try again.

MY COMMITMENT

I choose to..._____

_____

_____

_____

_____

I am grateful for... _____

_____

_____

_____

_____

_____

Service

Servant leadership – is there any other kind? When you are a leader, service to others should be your main intention. How can you lift others up? How do you come alongside them? How do you serve them?

GOAL
Can you find a webinar, YouTube video, or article that you could share with different members of your team that provides a unique development opportunity for them?

MY COMMITMENT

I choose to... _____

_____

_____

_____

_____

I am grateful for... _____

_____

_____

_____

_____

_____

Love

Remember the first time you fell in love? The butterflies.
The constant thoughts of that person. The hours on end of connection.
What if you had that same feeling about your work?
Your life? Your everyday?

GOAL
Dig deep into your memory and cherish that love stronghold.
Feel everything about it. Then live your day that way today (and everyday).

MY COMMITMENT

I choose to... _____

_____

_____

_____

_____

I am grateful for... _____

_____

_____

_____

_____

_____

Integrity

Do you do what you say you're going to do?
Are you walking the talk? Is integrity part of your moral compass?
Integrity makes up about 1/3 of the Trust Imperative Model.

GOAL
When you make a commitment today, stick with it regardless
of those small things that might sneak into your day.

MY COMMITMENT

I choose to... _____

_____

_____

_____

_____

I am grateful for... _____

_____

_____

_____

_____

_____

Encourage

As we make our way through a time of constant change, remember to encourage not only yourself to stay positive and flexible but also to give grace to your team and families.

GOAL

Give five supportive compliments today.
It could even be to a random person.

MY COMMITMENT

I choose to... _____

_____

_____

_____

_____

I am grateful for... _____

_____

_____

_____

_____

Empathy

There's a saying, "when you can be anything, be kind."
Remember, everyone is moving through today in their own way,
at their own pace and with their own set of challenges.

GOAL

Go old school, write a handwritten letter of hope to lift
someone else's spirits up. You don't even have to mail it;
you might drop it off on your daily walk.

MY COMMITMENT

I choose to... _____

_____

_____

_____

_____

I am grateful for... _____

_____

_____

_____

_____

_____

Belief

We need always to remind ourselves:
"I am whatever I believe me to be."

GOAL

Choose to self-motivate today. Look in the mirror and tell
yourself you are important and valuable. Find the truths of what you
believe you to be and own these truths proudly.

MY COMMITMENT

I choose to... _____

_____

_____

_____

_____

I am grateful for... _____

_____

_____

_____

_____

_____

BONUS WORD!

Give

It is important to give abundantly and receive graciously.

GOAL
If you were moved by this book, pay it forward and gift it to someone else.
Leadership Delta is gifting 15% of all net book sales towards
a scholarship for Delta Academy Leadership Forums.

MY COMMITMENT

I choose to... _____

_____

_____

_____

_____

I am grateful for... _____

_____

_____

_____

_____

_____

CPSIA information can be obtained
at www.ICGtesting.com
Printed in the USA
LVHW021454080121
675967LV00006B/287

9 781734 582932